An historical account of that venerable monument of antiquity the textus Roffensis; ... by Samuel Pegge ...

PRINT EDITIONS

Eighteenth Century
Collections Online
Print Editions

Gale ECCO Print Editions

Relive history with *Eighteenth Century Collections Online*, now available in print for the independent historian and collector. This series includes the most significant English-language and foreign-language works printed in Great Britain during the eighteenth century, and is organized in seven different subject areas including literature and language; medicine, science, and technology; and religion and philosophy. The collection also includes thousands of important works from the Americas.

The eighteenth century has been called "The Age of Enlightenment." It was a period of rapid advance in print culture and publishing, in world exploration, and in the rapid growth of science and technology – all of which had a profound impact on the political and cultural landscape. At the end of the century the American Revolution, French Revolution and Industrial Revolution, perhaps three of the most significant events in modern history, set in motion developments that eventually dominated world political, economic, and social life.

In a groundbreaking effort, Gale initiated a revolution of its own: digitization of epic proportions to preserve these invaluable works in the largest online archive of its kind. Contributions from major world libraries constitute over 175,000 original printed works. Scanned images of the actual pages, rather than transcriptions, recreate the works *as they first appeared.*

Now for the first time, these high-quality digital scans of original works are available via print-on-demand, making them readily accessible to libraries, students, independent scholars, and readers of all ages.

For our initial release we have created seven robust collections to form one the world's most comprehensive catalogs of 18th century works.

Initial Gale ECCO Print Editions collections include:

History and Geography
Rich in titles on English life and social history, this collection spans the world as it was known to eighteenth-century historians and explorers. Titles include a wealth of travel accounts and diaries, histories of nations from throughout the world, and maps and charts of a world that was still being discovered. Students of the War of American Independence will find fascinating accounts from the British side of conflict.

Social Science

Delve into what it was like to live during the eighteenth century by reading the first-hand accounts of everyday people, including city dwellers and farmers, businessmen and bankers, artisans and merchants, artists and their patrons, politicians and their constituents. Original texts make the American, French, and Industrial revolutions vividly contemporary.

Medicine, Science and Technology

Medical theory and practice of the 1700s developed rapidly, as is evidenced by the extensive collection, which includes descriptions of diseases, their conditions, and treatments. Books on science and technology, agriculture, military technology, natural philosophy, even cookbooks, are all contained here.

Literature and Language

Western literary study flows out of eighteenth-century works by Alexander Pope, Daniel Defoe, Henry Fielding, Frances Burney, Denis Diderot, Johann Gottfried Herder, Johann Wolfgang von Goethe, and others. Experience the birth of the modern novel, or compare the development of language using dictionaries and grammar discourses.

Religion and Philosophy

The Age of Enlightenment profoundly enriched religious and philosophical understanding and continues to influence present-day thinking. Works collected here include masterpieces by David Hume, Immanuel Kant, and Jean-Jacques Rousseau, as well as religious sermons and moral debates on the issues of the day, such as the slave trade. The Age of Reason saw conflict between Protestantism and Catholicism transformed into one between faith and logic -- a debate that continues in the twenty-first century.

Law and Reference

This collection reveals the history of English common law and Empire law in a vastly changing world of British expansion. Dominating the legal field is the *Commentaries of the Law of England* by Sir William Blackstone, which first appeared in 1765. Reference works such as almanacs and catalogues continue to educate us by revealing the day-to-day workings of society.

Fine Arts

The eighteenth-century fascination with Greek and Roman antiquity followed the systematic excavation of the ruins at Pompeii and Herculaneum in southern Italy; and after 1750 a neoclassical style dominated all artistic fields. The titles here trace developments in mostly English-language works on painting, sculpture, architecture, music, theater, and other disciplines. Instructional works on musical instruments, catalogs of art objects, comic operas, and more are also included.

The BiblioLife Network

This project was made possible in part by the BiblioLife Network (BLN), a project aimed at addressing some of the huge challenges facing book preservationists around the world. The BLN includes libraries, library networks, archives, subject matter experts, online communities and library service providers. We believe every book ever published should be available as a high-quality print reproduction; printed on-demand anywhere in the world. This insures the ongoing accessibility of the content and helps generate sustainable revenue for the libraries and organizations that work to preserve these important materials.

The following book is in the "public domain" and represents an authentic reproduction of the text as printed by the original publisher. While we have attempted to accurately maintain the integrity of the original work, there are sometimes problems with the original work or the micro-film from which the books were digitized. This can result in minor errors in reproduction. Possible imperfections include missing and blurred pages, poor pictures, markings and other reproduction issues beyond our control. Because this work is culturally important, we have made it available as part of our commitment to protecting, preserving, and promoting the world's literature.

GUIDE TO FOLD-OUTS MAPS and OVERSIZED IMAGES

The book you are reading was digitized from microfilm captured over the past thirty to forty years. Years after the creation of the original microfilm, the book was converted to digital files and made available in an online database.

In an online database, page images do not need to conform to the size restrictions found in a printed book. When converting these images back into a printed bound book, the page sizes are standardized in ways that maintain the detail of the original. For large images, such as fold-out maps, the original page image is split into two or more pages

Guidelines used to determine how to split the page image follows:

• Some images are split vertically; large images require vertical and horizontal splits.
• For horizontal splits, the content is split left to right.
• For vertical splits, the content is split from top to bottom.
• For both vertical and horizontal splits, the image is processed from top left to bottom right.

BIBLIOTHECA

TOPOGRAPHICA

BRITANNICA.

N° XXV.

CONTAINING

Mr. PEGGE's Hiftorical Account of the TEXTUS ROFFENSIS; and of Mr. ELSTOB and his SISTER.

WITH

MEMOIRS of Mr. JOHNSON, of CRANBROOKE.

[Price One Shilling and Six Pence.]

AMONG the various Labours of Literary Men, there have always been certain Fragments whose Size could not secure them a general Exemption from the Wreck of Time, which their intrinsic Merit entitled them to survive; but, having been gathered up by the Curious, or thrown into Miscellaneous Collections by Booksellers, they have been recalled into Existence, and by uniting together have defended themselves from Oblivion. Original Pieces have been called in to their Aid, and formed a Phalanx that might withstand every Attack from the Critic to the Cheesemonger, and contributed to the Ornament as well as Value of Libraries.

With a similar view it is here intended to present the Publick with some valuable Articles of BRITISH TOPOGRAPHY, from printed Books and MSS. One Part of this Collection will confist of Re-publications of scarce and various Tracts; another of such MS. Papers as the Editors are already possessed of, or may receive from their Friends.

It is therefore proposed to publish a Number occasionally, not confined to the same Price or Quantity of Sheets, nor always adorned with Cuts; but paged in such a Manner, that the general Articles, or those belonging to the respective Counties, may form a separate Succession, if there should be enough published, to bind in suitable Classes; and each Tract will be completed in a single Number.

Into this Collection all Communications consistent with the Plan will be received with Thanks. And as no Correspondent will be denied the Privilege of controverting the Opinions of another, so none will be denied Admittance without a fair and impartial Reason.

A N

HISTORICAL ACCOUNT

OF THAT VENERABLE

MONUMENT OF ANTIQUITY

THE TEXTUS ROFFENSIS;

INCLUDING

MEMOIRS of the learned SAXONISTS
Mr. WILLIAM ELSTOB and his SISTER.

By SAMUEL PEGGE, M.A.

To which are added,

Biographical Anecdotes of Mr. JOHNSON, Vicar of Cranbrooke;
and EXTRACTS from the REGISTERS of that PARISH.

———————————

LONDON,
PRINTED BY AND FOR J. NICHOLS,
PRINTER TO THE SOCIETY OF ANTIQUARIES;
AND SOLD BY ALL THE BOOKSELLERS IN GREAT BRITAIN AND IRELAND.
MDCCLXXXIV.

1784

An Historical Account of that venerable Monument of Antiquity
the TEXTUS ROFFENSIS.

[Read at the SOCIETY of ANTIQUARIES, London, June 18, 1767.]

THOUGH the hiſtory of a ſingle book may ſeem at firſt ſight to be both uncommon and trivial, yet when one conſiders the antiquity, and the great importance of the monument, commonly known by the name of TEXTUS ROFFENSIS [1]; the practice of our editors who are ſo careful and induſtrious, as to give us an exact account of every ſingle edition of the author they publiſh; and, laſtly, what has been lately done by Mr. Webb in his pamphlet concerning the record of Domeſday, the following narrative of the compilement, the contents, the fate, hiſtory, tranſcripts, and publications of this auguſt and moſt valuable remain, may not be altogether inſignificant or diſpleaſing; eſpecially as ſome things will ariſe that are very remarkable and intereſting.

I ſuppoſe we may ſafely depend upon Mr. Wharton, who, by the favour of the then dean and chapter of Rocheſter, had the book in his cuſtody for ſome time, for the author of it. He obſerves, that Ernulf [2], biſhop of Rocheſter, ſat in that ſee from A. D. 1114, to A. D. 1124, in the reign of king Henry I. and compiled the book, which is written in a very elegant hand. The biſhop was very old at the time, not leſs than 80, or 82; for

---

[1] In Dugdale's Monaſticon it is called *Chronicon Clauſtri Roffenſis*; and biſhop Godwin, in his Life of Ernulfus, ſpeaks of an Hiſtory of the Church of Rocheſter, left by Ernulfus, which I ſuppoſe is nothing but the **Textus**.
[2] He is otherwiſe written *Arnulf, Arnulph, Earnulph.*

hc

he was 84 when he died, A. D. 1124 [1], and yet the collection feems to have been made about 1120, according to Dr. Harris, in his Hiftory of Kent [2], or 1122 according to Mr. Hearne [3], and this latter I take to be the truer account; but as to Ernulf's being the author, an infcription in a very antient hand, in the front of the book, fuppofed by Mr. Wanley [4] to be no lefs than 400 years old, attefts the fame, *Textus de ecclefia Rofferfi per Ernulfum epifcopum* [5]; and it is obfervable, that there is nothing in the book of a later date than the time of the prelate here mentioned; for as to the 13 later archbifhops of Canterbury, and the 15 later bifhops of Rochefter, thefe have all been added by a more modern hand, as appears from the form of the letter, and the difference of the ink; one perfon added the 6 bifhops that followed Ernulf in fucceffion, and another, more recent, has added the 9 following them. To thefe may be added, fays Mr. Wharton, fome matters relative to the time of the bifhops, John and Afcelin, infcrted after the leaf 203; but all the reft of the book is written in a hand coeval with bifhop Ernulph [6].

In refpect of the contents of this famous MS. the book confifts of two parts; the firft containing the laws and conftitutions of the Anglo-Saxon kings, in Latin and Saxon, tranfcribed from ancient copies; and the fecond giving us a regifter or chartulary of the church of Rochefter, from the autographs, with fome other matters relating to that cathedral, written in the times of Ernulf and his fucceffors; but thefe laft in a later hand. Bifhop

[1] Hearne in his *Prafatio*, Wharton, and Gul. Malmfb. p. 234.

[2] Pag. 32. Dr. Harris though varies from himfelf in this refpect, for in a note inferted by him in the original at Rochefter, on the reverfe of the fecond leaf, he conjectures the *text* might be compiled A. D. 1115, which is not fo credible.

[3] See his *Prafatio*, p. xxxv.

[4] Dr. Hickes's Thef. tom. III. p. 273.

[5] Text⁹ de eccē Roffñ per Ernultū Epm̄ Mr. Wanley, l. c.

[6] Mr. Wharton's Angl. Sacr. tom. I. p. xxx. feq.

Ernulf

Ernulf was a Norman [1]; and, in regard to the firft part of
the work, Mr. Hearne applauds him extremely for his great
diligence and application, in making himfelf mafter of the
Saxon language then growing into difufe, and his commendable
care in preferving and perpetuating this momentous code. The
above fhort account of the contents is taken from Mr. Wanley,
in whom may be feen, by thofe who are defirous of it, a very
exact lift of all the articles that compofe the firft part, with a
general reprefentation fuperadded of what is to be found in the
fecond. I fhall content myfelf with giving the following ab-
breviation from Mr. Wharton; 'The laws of Ethelbert, Ælfred,
'Guthrun, Edward the Elder, Edmund, and Ethelred, in Saxon [2].
'The exorcifm of the Ordeal, the laws of K. Cnut, the con-
'ftitutions of William I. Extracts from the decrees of the Popes,
'the inftitutions of K. Henry I. A. D. 1101, the fucceffion of
'the Popes and Emperors, of the Patriarchs of Jerufalem, and
'the other four patriarchal fees [3], the names of the archbifhops
'and bifhops of England, from the time of Auguftin the monk,
'diftributed according to their fees, in Latin. *Judicia civitatis*
'*London* [4], the genealogy of K. Edward the Confeffor from
'Adam, the genealogies of all the kings of the Heptarchy from
'Adam [5], in Saxon. The privileges, charters, and ordinances
'of the church of Rochefter, in Latin and Saxon.' Bifhop

[1] Whoever defires a further account of him may confult Malmfbury, Mr.
Hearne's Preface, p. xiv. and Appendix, N I. II. III. IV. Wharton, A S. tom I.
p. 35. Bifhop Tanner's Biblioth. Gunton's Hiftory of Peterborough, Cave's Hift.
Lit. &c.

[2] Thefe are far from being all.

[3] Rather *the other three*, for there were but 5 in all, and thofe of Rome and
Jerufalem are mentioned before. However, there are only two in the original, Alexandria and Antioch.

[4] Thefe are laws of K. Athelftan; they are extant in Brompton inter X Script.
col. 852. and in Wilkins; fee alfo bifhop Nicolfon's Hift. Libr. p 14.

[5] i. e. they are carried up to Woden, who in the former is carried up to Adam.

Nicolfon's

Nicolfon's account of this matter is still fhorter; but, as he mentions fome things neverthelefs, omitted by Wharton, I fhall infert it. ' It furnifhes us,' fays he, ' with the laws of four ' Kentifh kings (Ethelbert, Hlothere, Eadhed [1], and Withred) ' omitted by Lambard [2], together with the Saxon form of oaths ' of fealty, and wager of law; the old form of curfing by bell, ' book, and candle; of Ordale, &c.' [3]

I enter now upon the fate, hiftory, tranfcripts, and impreffions of this book, and its parts.

The firft perfon that made any ufe of our MS. fince the reftoration of learning, was that great reviver of Saxon literature, Lawrence Nowell archdeacon of Derby, and dean of Lichfield. The famous Kentifh antiquary William Lambarde was a difciple of his in the Saxon tongue, of which he is reckoned the fecond reftorer [4]; and the dean having made certain tranfcripts from the Textus, imparted them to him, giving him withal other affiftance, and the ufe of his notes, towards the completing his Archæonomia [5]; he alfo gave him his Vocabularium Saxonicum [6], and died A. D. 1577 [7].

The abovementioned Mr. Lambarde publifhed his Archæonomia, A. D. 1568, in quarto, wherein are various tranfcripts from this MS. But thefe, as Dr. Hickes has clearly fhewn [8], were not copied by him from the original book, which he did not fee till the year 1573, when his name occurs in the margin of it, as

[1] *Eadric,* as I fuppofe.
[2] Meaning in the Archæonomia.
[3] Nicolfon, Hift. Libr. p. 134.
[4] Wood, Hift. & Antiq. Lib. II. p. 216.
[5] Wood, Ath. I col. 186.
[6] Tanner, Bibl. p. 554.
[7] Bifhop Tanner fays, 1576; but fee Dr. Br. Willis's Cath. tom. I. p. 400. Mr. Wood is doubtful where he is buried, unlefs at Lichfield; but Dr. Willis rather thinks it was at Wefton in Derbyfhire.
[8] Hickes, Epift. to Sir Barth. Shower in 2d tome of his Thef. p. 88.

it does in various places, but they were put into his hands by his preceptor the dean of Lichfield, and he published them in this volume with his own English translation.

Archbishop Matthew Parker, and his Assistant John Josceline [1], appear next to have used our MS. for the Antiq. Brit. Ecclef. being printed A. 1572. *Lib. Roff.* is often cited in the margin.

Afterwards, A. D. 1576, Mr. Lambarde's first edition of the Perambulation of Kent appeared; and there we have an extract printed from our MS. concerning the maintenance and support of Rochester Bridge, in Saxon and Latin; the Saxon being also translated by him into modern English [2]. It occurs also in Elstob's transcript to be mentioned below, and in Mr. Hearne's Appendix, p. 379. Archdeacon Denne has also transcribed the Latin part into his copy of Hearne's edition; and you have the Latin, Saxon, and English, in Dr. Harris's History of Kent, p. 260. Mr. Lambarde cites the MS. again, p. 271. 317. and 343. of this first edition. He has also there printed Brihtric's will, p. 357, from it, though he has not noted that, and has given us an English translation of it. This curious monument has likewise appeared in Dr. Hickes's Thesaurus [3], both in Saxon and Latin; in Hearne's Textus Roffensis, p. 110, you have the Saxon part, and in the preface, p. xxv. the Saxon with Mr. Lambarde's English version; as likewise in Dr. Harris's History of Kent, p. 201.

A. D. 1623, Mr. Selden published the Monkish Historian Eadmer; and in the Spicilegium, 197, has printed from this MS. the famous pleading at Pinnenden Heath, near Maidstone in Kent (now called Pickenden Heath), between archbishop Lanfranc and Odo bishop of Baieux, in Latin. This hath been many times reprinted since, as by Sir William Dugdale in his

[1] Of whom, fee the History of Lambeth Palace.
[2] Perambul p. 307, feq edit. 1576. The Author's 2d Edition of this book was published A. 1596. which is an enlarged, and the best edition.
[3] Tom. II. in Epist. ad Barth. Shower, p. 51. See also tom. III. p. 241.

Origines Jurid. Mr. Wharton, in Anglia Sacra, tom. I. p. 334; and laftly, by Dr. Harris, in his Hiftory of Kent, p. 50.

A. D. 1626, came out the firft part of Sir Henry Spelman's Gloffary; and therein he inferted from this MS. the old form of excommunication, or curfing by bell, book, and candle [1]. This appears alfo in Mr. Hearne's edition of the Textus, p. 55.

The book, after this, was in the utmoft danger of being fecreted, and finally eftranged from the church, before half of it had been either printed or tranfcribed; one Leonard, a doctor of phyfick, had got it into his hands, and kept it two years; but the dean, Walter Balcanqual, and the chapter, getting fcent of the purloiner, beftirred themfelves, and at laft recovered their MS. but not without a bill in chancery. Concerning this tranfaction, the following note is now entered on the 2d leaf: ' Venerandum hoc antiquitatis monumentum per integrum bien- ' nium defideratum, furreptore tandem detecto, ac reftitutionem ' ftrenue negante, decreto fupremæ curiæ, quam cancellariam ' vocant, non exiguis hujus ecclefiæ fumptibus, recuperavit, red- ' dique priftinis dominis curavit Gualterus Balcanqual hujus ' ecclefiæ decanus anno poft natum incarnatum 1633.' This memorandum, which is alfo copied by Mr. Wanley in Dr. Hickes's Thef. tom. III. p. 273. is now pafted on the 2d folio, and is probably the hand-writing of dean Balcanqual; it is alfo anew tranfcribed with the following note, *This is written on the wooden cover of this book, and thence copied by J. H. D. D. P R.* that is, John Harris, D. D. Prebendary of Rochefter. It appears clearly from Hearne's Preface, p. vi. that Dr. Leonard was the pilferer, for he had the book in his keeping, A. D. 1632.

[1] We read there, *In dentibus mord cibus, in labris, fi e moli'ris;* and fo Mr Hearne gives it alfo, p 58. but certainly we ought to read, *in labris fæ mol ribus.* It is the fault of the original fcribe, for Dr. Denne has not corrected it in his book to be mentioned below.

Whilft

Whilst the book was in Dr. Leonard's custody [1], Sir Edward Deiing, the first baronet of the family, a gentleman of great parts and learning, and of immense application, made a transcript with his own hand [2] of the whole of this book, that had not been already printed, or was not expected to be printed [3], which will be again mentioned below; and this he did with a public-spirited design of having it pass the press. Sir Edward's hand is seen often in the margin of the original book; and from one place it appears, that he had recourse to the book, A. D. 1644, the very year he died, and after the MS. had been recovered into the hands of the dean and chapter.

The first volume of Sir Henry Spelman's Councils came out A. D. 1639; wherein he has inserted several transcripts from this MS. but it is a question whether he ever saw the original; for hear what Mr. Johnson says, ' By this inspection (of the MS. ' in relation to K. Wihtred's laws) I further learned, that Sir H. ' Spelman did most probably never view the MS. itself. For there ' are some mistakes so very gross, that none used to the reading ' of Saxon monuments could possibly be guilty of them The ' transcript from which he published them seems to have been ' made by some one that was a stranger to the Saxonic letters [4].'

A. D. 1640, John de Laet, a celebrated scholar of Antwerp, translated the laws of Ethelbert, Hlothere and Eadrie, into Latin. He never saw the original, but had a transcript sent him by Sir Henry Spelman; and the original Saxon, with its version, may be seen in Dr. Hickes's Thesaurus [5].

---

[1] Hearne's Præfat. p. v.
[2] So I understand Mr. Hearne.
[3] However, there were many things in this transcript that had been already published, as appears from Hearne's edition of it.
[4] Johnson's Pref. to Collection of Laws, &c. p. iii.
[5] Tom. II. in the Dissert. Epist. p. 88. seq.

Abraham

Abraham Whelock, Arabic Profeſſor and public Librarian at Cambridge, reprinted Mr. Lambarde's Archæonomia, A. 1644, in folio.   He had the uſe of a copy of Mr. Lambarde's edition, amended in various places by the editor [1], and moreover made ſeveral additions to the work.

I ſuppoſe it might be about the time that Mr. Somner collated Sir Henry Spelman's firſt volume of Councils, in the articles taken from the *Textus*, with the original; for that he compared the printed book therewith, we learn from Mr. Johnſon [2] and biſhop Kennet's Life of Mr. Somner [3].   The volume ſo emended by him is now in the library of the church of Canterbury, and has been made uſe of by Dr. Wilkins.

During the time of the grand rebellion, biſhop Nicolſon ſuppoſes, this book was wiſely committed to the care of Sir Roger Twyſden, one of the learned editors of the X Scriptores; for in his cuſtody, he ſays, he found it often referred to by Sir William Dugdale, in a work which he compoſed during theſe troubles [4].

A. D. 1655, the firſt volume of Sir William Dugdale's Monaſticon came out, wherein Mr. Dodſworth and he have made good uſe of our MS.

A. D. 1664, the ſecond edition of Sir H. Spelman's Gloſſary was publiſhed; this contained the entire work, of which the former part had been corrected and enlarged by the author; and in the new, or ſecond part, are inſerted the forms of the ordeal trials, from our MS. which were alſo in Sir Edward Dering's tranſcript, and have ſince appeared both in Mr. Hearne's edition of that tranſcript, and in Mr. Browne's Faſciculus to be mentioned below.   It ought to be here noted, that though this ſecond part of

[1] Hickes's Theſ. ibid. p. 87.
[2] Johnſon's Pref. to Collection of Laws, &c. p. ii.
[3] Biſhop Kennet's Life of Mr. Somner, prefixed to Somner's Roman ports and forts, p. 89.
[4] He means Sir William's Orig. Jurid.   See Nic. Hiſt. Libr. p. 134.

the

the Glossary did not appear till anno 1664, yet it was compiled at the time the first part was, as we are informed in the preface to the last and best edition, printed A. D. 1687.

A. D. 1666, Sir William Dugdale's *Origines Juridiciales* appeared, into which he copied from our MS. as mentioned above, the famous pleading at Pinnenden Heath, having made use of the MS. whilst it was lodged in the hand of Sir Roger Twysden.

Mr. Edward Browne, the worthy and learned rector of Sundrich in Kent, reprinted the *Fasciculus rerum expetendarum et fugiendarum*, anno 1689, in folio; and in the Appendix, or vol. II. p 903, the *Officium Ordalii* is printed, as transcribed by him from the original MS. [1]

A. D. 1691, Mr. Wharton published his *Anglia Sacra* in two tomes, folio. The dean and chapter of Rochester intrusted him with their MS. to Lambeth, where Mr. Wharton then resided as chaplain to archbishop Sancroft, and from thence he has transmitted into his first volume, p. 329, seq. whatever was suitable to his present design; and this was the first publication of this part of the MS.

In the same year, came out Dr. Gale's *Hist. Brit. Sax. Anglo Daniæ Scriptores* XV. and p. 792. he has inserted from our own MS. *Genealogias per partes in Britannia regum regnari*, which he styles a rare monument, *formerly* transcribed by him from this very ancient book. Charles Bertram, of Copenhagen, has since reprinted these Genealogies from Dr. Gale's edition, in his *Brit. Gent. Hist. antiq. Scriptores Tres*, printed at Copenhagen, anno 1757 [2]. A part of these genealogies appear also in Hearne's edition of Sir Edward Dering's Transcript, p. 60, and the whole of them in that Transcript which was made by the Elstobs. See below.

[1] See above, A. D. 1664.
[2] See the Preface prefixed there to Nennius.

C

Di.

Dr. Hickes, in the fecond tome of his Thefaurus publifhed anno 1703, obliged the world with his famous *Differtatio Epiflolaris ad Bartholomæum Showere*. The doctor was a perfon of, great accuracy, and had recourfe to the original MS. not only for the pieces already mentioned, but likewife for feveral others, which he has given us in that excellent epiftle.

In 1705, Mr. Humphrey Wanley's large Catalogue of the northern books, both printed and MS. came out, making the third volume to Dr. Hickes's Thefaurus; and here, p. 273. f q. we have a lift of all the articles contained in our MS. as mentioned above, from his own ocular infpection.

A. D. 1712. the MS. was at London, and, I imagine, for the ufe of Dr. Harris, who was prebendary of Rochefter, and was then upon his Hiftory of Kent; for though this work did not appear till anno 1719, yet he had begun it, as he tells us, eight years before. Mr. Johnfon was defirous of collating Sir H. Spelman's edition of K. Wihtred's laws, with the original, but in a complaining ftrain tells us; 'That noble MS. was not at 'home in its proper repofitory, during the whole time that I was ' compofing this work '.' The work came out A. D. 1720, being his Collection of Laws, &c. However, the MS. was now in London; for the rev. Mr. William Elftob, and his fifter Mrs. Elizabeth Elftob, employed one James Smith, a boy of ten years old, to make a tranfcript for them, in folio, of fuch parts of the MS. as had not been before publifhed '. This tranfcript the brother and fifter collated and examined together, and it was finifhed x kal. June, or 23 May, 1712, being very fairly written in three months time; and a very extraordinary performance it is for fuch a boy. Every page of it anfwers to the

---

' Mr. Johnfon's general preface to his Collection of Laws, &c.

' There are fome things neverthelefs in this tranfcript that had been printed before, as is noted above in feveral places.

pages

pages of the original book: and as what it contains more than the Dering tranfcript printed by Mr. Hearne will be noted hereafter; I fhall only obferve here, that this tranfcript, on the death of Mr. Elftob, came into the hands of his uncle, Dr. Charles Elftob, prebendary of Canterbury; and when he died, it was purchafed with the reft of Mr. William Elftob's Saxon tranfcripts by Mr. Jofeph Ames, fecretary to the Society of Antiquaries at London; and I bought it at his auction, anno 1760.

But this Mr. William Elftob, and his learned fifter, being perfons not generally known, though both of them exceedingly eminent in their way, I fhall here infert a fhort account of them, from the papers of the fifter, who, about the year 1738, compiled a brief Narrative of her own and her brother's Life, and gave it in her own hand-writing to Mr. George Ballard, whom we fhall often have occafion to mention hereafter, and at whofe requeft fhe drew it up. Dr. Nathanael Wetherell, the worthy mafter of Univerfity College, was fo fortunate as to find the narrative among Mr. Ballard's MSS. in the Bodleian Library, and fent a tranfcript of it to the honourable and right reverend the Lord Bifhop of Carlifle, who was pleafed to communicate it to me, in order to enable me to give the following authentic, though contracted, account.

William Elftob was born January the firft, fixteen hundred and feventy-three, at Newcaftle upon Tyne. He was the fon of Ralph Elftob [1], merchant in that place, who was defcended from a very ancient family in the bifhoprick of Durham [2]; as appears not only from their pedigree in the Heralds Office, but from feveral writings now in the family, one of which is a grant from William de la More, mafter of the Knights Templars, to Adam

---

[1] By Jane his wife; Mrs. Elftob's own Life. S. P.

[2] See the notes on the Homily on St. Gregory's Day, p. 17. The name is alfo there accounted for, p. 16. S. P.

de

d Elneſtob, in the year thirteen hundred and four, on condition of their paying twenty-four ſhillings to their houſe at Shotton, *et faciendo duos conventus ad curiam ſuam de Foxdene.*

William had the earlieſt part of his education at Newcaſtle [2], from thence at about eleven years of age he removed to Eaton, where he continued five years. From Eaton, by the advice of an uncle, who was his guardian [3], he was placed at Catherine Hall in Cambridge, in a ſtation below his birth and fortune. THis, and the air not agreeing with his conſtitution, which was conſumptive, was the occaſion of his removal to Queen's College, Oxford, under the tuition of Dr. Maugh, where he was a commoner, and continued till he was elected fellow of Univerſity College, by the friendſhip of Dr. Charlett, maſter of that college, Dr. Hudſon, &c. [4].

In ſeventeen hundred and two, he was by the dean and chapter of Canterbury preſented to the united pariſhes of St. Swithin and St. Mary Bothaw, in London [5], where, after he had diſcharged the duty of a faithful and orthodox paſtor, with great patience and reſignation, after a long and lingering illneſs, he exchanged this life for a better, on Saturday, March the third, ſeventeen hundred and fourteen-fifteen [6].

[1] I ſhould ſuppoſe from hence that the grant ran to Adam de Elneſtob, and his heirs. S. P

[2] Where his father was ſheriff, anno 1685. Bourne's Hiſtory of Newcaſtle, p. 243. S P.

[3] Charles Elſtob, D D. who was inſtalled prebendary of Canterbury, anno 1685, and there died, anno 17.1. S. P.

[4] He removed to Univerſity College, 23 July, 1696, and was elected Fellow the ſame year, being then Bachelor of Arts. June 8, 1697, he took the degree of Maſter. Catalogue of Graduates at Oxford, 1727, 8vo. S. P.

[5] By the procurement, no doubt, of his uncle the prebendary. St Mary Bothaw, after the fire of London, was united to St. Swithin; and as the dean and chapter of Canterbury were patrons of the former, and the Salters Company of the latter, the two incorporations have an alternate patronage, and the turn at this time was in the dean and chapter; the livings together are reputed at 140 l. per annum. S. P.

[6] And was buried in the chancel of St. Swithin's Church, London, under the communion table. S. P.

1

Mrs.

Mrs. Elstob informed Mr. Ballard by letter, that her brother was chaplain to William Nicolson, bishop of Carlisle[1]. Nicolson was consecrated 14 June, 1702, and it was probably soon after that, that he was appointed chaplain, but I imagine he was only titularly, and not domestically so. However, in February 1713, upon a prospect of a vacancy at Lincoln's Inn, on the promotion of Dr. Francis Gastrel to the see of Chester, he solicited lord chief justice Parker for his interest, that he might be appointed preacher there. He intimates in his letter[2], that he had not met with success in the world answerable to his merits; and it is certain he had not, nor was he more fortunate in the present application. The character which the lady gives of her brother, and which the reader would probably like best to receive in her own words, runs thus:

'To his parents, while they lived, he was a most dutiful son,
' affectionate to his relations, a most sincere friend, very chari-
' table to the poor, a kind master to his servants, and generous
' to all, which was his greatest fault. He was of so sweet a
' temper, that hardly any thing could make him shew his resent-
' ment, but when any thing was said or done to the prejudice of
' religion, or disadvantage of his country.

' He had what might justly be called an universal genius, no
' arts or sciences being despised by him: he had a particular
' genius for languages, and was a master of the Greek and
' Latin; of the latter he was esteemed a good judge, and to
' write it with great purity; nor was he ignorant of the Oriental
' languages, as well as the Septentrional. He was a great lover

---

[1] Ballard's addition to Mrs Elstob's account of her brother.

[2] In the letter he wrote to the lord chief justice on the occasion, which is now in the hands of my most obliging friend Thomas Astle, esq; he observes, ' he had been
' a preacher in the city eleven years, and diligent in his profession, as well as la-
' borious in other matters, without seeking or finding such assistances as are both
' useful and necessary to such as converse with books.'

' of

' of the antiquities of other countries, but more especially those
' of our own, having been at the pains and expences of visiting
' most of the places in this nation that are remarkable either for
' natural or antient curiosities, architecture, paintings, sculp-
' ture, &c.

' What time he could spare from the study of divinity, was
' spent chiefly in the Saxon learning, in which he was a great
' proficient.'

Mrs. Elstob, after this, proceeds to give a detail of her
brother's Works; but as she is very short upon this subject, and
indeed has not mentioned them all, I shall here exhibit an enlarged description of them, partly from my own observations,
and the information of Dr. Wetherell, but principally from Mr.
Ballard's MS. Preface to his own transcript of king Ælfred's
Anglo-Saxon version of Orosius, communicated to me by the
most benevolent and public-spirited bishop of Carlisle.

Mr. Elstob was a person extremely well versed in the Saxon
tongue ', and being then resident in college, the very learned
Dr. Hickes solicited him to give a Latin translation of the Saxon
Homily of Lupus, and prevailed.   The original, with the Latin
version, is inserted by the doctor in his Epistolary Dissertation
abovementioned, p. 99. seq.   The Epistle Dedicatory to Doctor
Hickes, thereunto prefixed, is dated University College, v Id.
or 9 August, 1701; Mr. Elstob being then joint tutor in the
College with Dr. Clavering, late bishop of Peterborough, and in
possession of a transcript of the original Saxon made by Junius,
to which he hath not only added the Latin version beforementioned, but also many excellent notes. He styles it " the first fruits
" of his labours in the Saxon tongue."

' In Literatura et Antiquitate Septentrionali præclare eruditus Willielmus Elstob
Coll. gii Universitatis apud Oxonienses socius dignissimus. Hickesius, in Dissert.
Lp.il. p. 98.

Mr.

Mr. Elſtob was author of ' An Eſſay on the great affinity and 'mutual agreement of the two profeſſions of Divinity and Law, 'and on the joint intereſt of Church and State, in vindication of 'the Clergy's concerning themſelves in Political Matters.' Lond. 92 pages 8vo. To this, his friend Dr. Hickes wrote a Preface of two pages [1], on which occaſion I may be allowed to obſerve, that he maintained an intimacy and correſpondence alſo with the learned Mr. Humphrey Wanley [2], was well known to Dr. John Batteley, archdeacon of Canterbury, and to Sir Andrew Fountaine, who, reciting the names of thoſe that had furniſhed him with Saxon coins for his tables, ſpeaks of Mr. Elſtob in the following terms : ' Nec non reverendus magiſter Elſtob, qui pro ' eximia ſua humanitate mihi communicavit Iconas nummorum, ' quos ipſe habet Saxonicorum et quidem rariſſimorum ; atque ' etiam copiam mihi fecit nummorum, quos poſſidet reverendus ' C. (lege J.) Batteley archidiaconus Cantuarienſis ; ſed dolendum ' eſt, hoſce omnes ad me haud prius delatos eſſe, quam exculptæ ' fuerint tabulæ ; nec interim licere eoſdem commode tabulis in- ' ferere ; cum fuerint omnes nummi regis Ethelredi, modo unum ' excipias qui erat Ethelſtani, et quatuor qui erant Edmundi [3].' To the above learned authors and antiquaries, I may add the great lawyers, John Forteſcue Aland, Eſq; and lord chief juſtice Parker [4]. As to Mr. Strype, Mr. Elſtob ſeems to have cultivated

an

---

[1] Thoreſby, Ducat Leod. p. 129. and the MS. Life by Mrs. Eſtob. Hence he ſays to lord chief juſtice Parker in the letter above mentioned : ' Your lordſhip's ' kind opinion of the reſpect I have for the Engliſh laws will, I hope, make this ' addreſs at leaſt not impertinent.' Indeed his ſentiments on this head are moſt evident from his deſign hereafter to be mentioned, of publiſhing a new edition of the Saxon Laws.

[2] He calls Mr. Wanley in the MS. Oroſius mentioned below, *Amicus noſter per-humanus doctiſſimuſque*. This is extremely natural, as Wanley had been a ſtudent in Univerſity College. See Hickes Theſ. III. p. 90.

[3] Sir Andrew Fountaine, in Diſſert. epiſtol. præmiſſ. tabulis numm. Sax. p. 166.

[4] He begins the letter to lord chief juſtice Parker thus : ' Your lordſhip was ' pleaſed to do me a great deal of honour when I was permitted to wait upon you

' with

an early acquaintance with him : He communicated to Mr. Elftob a copy of an inedited epiftle of Roger Afcham's [1], and Llftob in return tranflated for him the mutilated Difcourfe of Sir John Cheke on Superftition [2], printed with Mr. Elftob's letter to Mr. Strype, prefixed to Strype's Life of Cheke.

Before Mr. Elftob left Oxford, he printed a neat edition of the celebrated Roger Afcham's Epiftles ; to which he fubjoined the letters of John Sturmius, Hieron. Oforius, and others, to Afcham and other Englifh gentlemen, Oxford, 1703; 8vo. He dedicates it to Robert Heath, Efq; his familiar friend, to whom he had been affiftant in his ftudies [3].

Soon after he was fettled in his benefice at London, he publifhed ' A Sermon upon the Thankfgiving for the Victory ob-
' tained by her Majefty's forces, and thofe of her allies, over
' the French and Bavarians near Hoehftet, under the conduct
' of his Grace the Duke of Marlborough. London, 1704.' The text was Pf. CIII. 10. Alfo,

' A Sermon on the Anniverfary Thankfgiving for her Majefty's
' happy Acceffion to the Throne. London, 1704.' The text 1 Tim. ii. 1, 2.

Sir John Cheke tranflated Plutarch's book on Superftition into Latin, and premifed a Difcourfe of his own upon that fubject in the Latin tongue. A caftrated copy of this Difcourfe, after it had lain long in obfcurity, was difcovered by Mr. Elftob in the Library of Univerfity College ; and he, as Mr. Strype tells us, not only courteoufly tranfcribed it for his ufe, but alfo voluntarily took the pains of tranflating it into Englifh [4]. The verfion

---

' with Mr. Fortefcue ; the learned converfation, and kind treatment, and generous
' promifes of favour, by which you then made me your lordfhip's debtor, call for
' my largeft acknowledgments, &c.'
[1] Elftob's edition of Afcham's Epiftles, p. 379.
[2] See below. [3] See the Dedication.
[4] Advertifement prefixed to Strype's Life of Sir John Cheke.

is accordingly printed at the end of Strype's Life of Sir John Cheke, London, 1705, 8vo. There is a particular concerning this piece of Cheke's, which is well worth noting ; several pages, believed to contain the arguments of the author against the various superstitions of the Church of Rome, are wanting in the original; and Mr. Elstob, who always entertained a thorough detestation of the Popish innovations in religion, supposes, with reason, that those sheets were surreptitiously taken out of the work by the famous Obadiah Walker, when he was master of University College, and had power over the MS, in the reign of king James II. The Papists, as he observes, being remarkable for their clean conveyances that way [1].

In 1709, his Latin version of the Saxon Homily on St. Gregory's Day, which he presented to his learned sister in a short Latin epistle, was printed at the end of her fine edition of the Saxon original.

' Mr. Elstob has published [2],' they are the words of Mr. Ballard, ' the larger devotions which the Saxons made use of at
' that time in their own language, which from probable con-
' jectures he fancies was the performance either of Ælfric arch-
' bishop of Canterbury, or of Wolfstan archbishop of York [3].
' And to shew the world that they did not contain any thing but
' what is pure and orthodox, he has obliged the public with a
' faithful translation of them [4].'

We are informed by his accomplished sister, that Mr. Elstob had made a collection of materials towards a history of his native place ; that he had collected a vast number of proper

---

[1] Elstob's Letter to Strype, in Strype's Life of Cheke, where by *Ob.* is meant *Obadiah Walker*, as is evident from p. 275.
[2] At the end of the first volume of Dr. Hickes's Letters which passed between him and a Popish priest. London, 1715, 8vo.
[3] See Mr. Elstob's Letter to Dr. Hickes, prefixed to the Devotions.
[4] Mr. Ballard's MS. Preface to Orosius, mentioned above.

D   names

names of men and women formerly ufed in northern countries; and that he likewife wrote an Effay concerning the Latin tongue, with a fhort account of its hiftory and ufe, for the encouragement of fuch adult perfons to fet upon the learning of it, who have either neglected, or been frightened from receiving the benefit of that kind of education in their infancy; to which is added, fome advice for the moft eafy and fpeedy attainment of it. What is become of the two collections above-mentioned, is uncertain, and not very material; but as Mr. Elftob was a moft excellent Latinift, his obfervations on that language muft have been highly acceptable to the public, and one has reafon to regret the lofs of them.

But the moft confiderable of Mr. Elftob's defigns, was an edition of the Saxon Laws, of which Mr. Ballard writes thus: ' Mr. ' Elftob had fpent much time and pains in preparing for the ' prefs a very valuable edition of all the Saxon Laws, both in ' print and manufcripts, of which learned performance, there is ' a great character given both by Dr. Hickes in his dedication ' prefixed to his firft volume of Sermons, and by John Fortefcue ' Aland, efq; in his preface to the book of *abfolute and unlimited* ' ' *Monarchy.* But as the propo_als for that work are fallen into ' my hands; and as they will give a more perfect idea of the ' performance, I will here add a tranfcript of them.

' Propofals in order to a new edition of the Saxon Laws.

' I. That thofe Laws which Mr. Lambarde and Mr. Whelock ' publifhed, be publifhed again more correctly.

' II. That the Laws of king Etheberht, with thofe of Edric ' and Hlotharius, and whatever elfe of that kind is to be met ' with, either in the *Textus Roffenfis,* or in any other ancient MSS. ' judged proper to be inferted, be alfo added.

' Read *limited.*

' III. That

' III. That that of J. Brompton, and the most ancient Tranf-
' lations, be confidered and compared, and, if thought conve-
' nient, be likewife printed.

' IV. That an entire new Latin tranflation be added of Mr.
' Somner's.

' V. That fuch various readings, references, and annotations,
' of learned men, viz. Spelman, Selden, Junius, D'Ewes, Laet,
' Hickes, &c. be adjoined, as fhall ferve to illuftrate the work ;
' with what other obfervations occur to the editor, untouched by
' thefe learned men.

' VI. A general preface, giving an account of the original
' and progrefs of the Englifh Laws to the Norman Conqueft,
' and thence to Magna Charta.

' VII. That there be particular prefaces, giving fo far an
' account of the feveral kings, as concerned their making Laws.

' VIII. An addition of proper gloffaries and indexes ".'

The death of Mr. Elftob prevented, as Mr. Ballard fays, the
publication of this ufeful performance, concerning which, fee
Mr. Thorefby's *Ducatus Leod.* p. 129. and Dr. Wilkins's *Præf.
ad Leges Sax.* But this is the lefs to be lamented, as the learned
Dr. David Wilkins, prebendary of Canterbury, has fince obliged
the world with a work of the fame kind, as will be mentioned
hereafter ; and yet I think Mr. Elftob's defign promifed to be
more copious and large than the Doctor's, especially in refpect
of annotation and elucidation.

He was prevented alfo by death in another project, which was
to give us king Ælfred's paraphraftical Saxon verfion of the
Latin Hiftorian Orofius. Notice of this intention we have from
Dr. Hickes, who, fpeaking of Mr. Elftob, fays, ' Ælfredi R.
' qui collegium fundarit, verfionem Orofii libri hiftoriarum, qui

----

' Mr. Ballard's MS. Preface cited above.

' et

'ev Ormesta divinam, Deo sospitante, literario orbi aliquando
'etiam daturus'. Our author had proceeded so far in this work
as to make a fair copy of it with his own hand in the Bodleian
Library, anno 1698, when he was very young, from a transcript of Junius's taken from a MS. in the Cotton Library, Ti-
berius B. E. Dr. Marshal afterwards collated Junius's transcript
with the MS. in the Lauderdale Library, which had formerly
belonged to Dr. Dee; and Mr. Elstob's copy is collated with the
MS. in the Cotton Library, and there is also mention in the said
copy of the Hatton MS. But this work, though it had been so
long and so well prepared [3], was never put to the press, but
came into the hands of Mr. Joseph Ames, at whose auction I
bought it. Here it may be pertinent to note, that Mr. George
Ballard, of Campden, in Gloucestershire, made another copy
from Junius's MS. A. D. 1751, in 4to. and prefixed a large
preface, shewing the use and advantages of the Anglo-Saxon
literature. This volume, which is very fairly written. Mr.
Ballard bequeathed by will to Dr. Charles Lyttelton, Bishop of
Carlisle, then Dean of Exeter, to whom the copy is addressed,
and his lordship was so condescending as to favour me with
the perusal of it, and I have drawn considerable helps from the

---

[1] This word is thought to be a corruption of *de miseria mundi* See Professor *Haver-
camp's* Preface to his edition; but rather perhaps of *orbis miseria*, written abbreviately
in the old exemplar, whence the MSS. in being were taken. *Or. misia,* and misread
by the copyers *Ormesta.*

[2] Hickesii Differt. Epist. ad Barth. Shower, p. 98.

[3] Mr. Elstob, speaking of the method he had used in translating the Saxon
Homily abovementioned, says, he had done it, ' iildem fere verbis repositis qua in
' Saxonica olim transfusa, vel ex Turonensi Gregorio, vel tuo, vel ex Beda nostrate
' vel utroque Diacono, et Johanne et Paulo. *Eadem plane rations, qua jam pridem*
' OROSIUM *a nobis elucubratum sos.*' Epist. ad sororem, præmiss. Lat. vers. Homiliæ
Saxonicæ, whence it should seem he had added a body of notes upon Orosius in a
volume separate from the copy he had made of the Saxon version, for nothing of
this kind appears in the copy. Perhaps they were intended to be transcribed into
the blank leaves at the end of the copy, which are numerous.

3   preface

preface relative to Mr. Elftob and his learned fifter, as appears above, and will be further evident in the fequel. Both Dr. Marfhal and Mr. Ballard [1] feem to have had it in their intention to publifh the Saxon verfion of Orofius [2]; but, however that was, the cafe is clear in regard to Mr. Elftob, concerning whom Mr. Ballard writes, ' It is very certain that the reverend and learned ' Mr. Elftob tranfcribed it with that view, and accordingly ' printed a fpecimen of it, which I have feen ; it bore the fol- ' lowing title. HORMESTA PAULI OROSII *quam olim patrio fer-* ' *mone donavit* ÆLFREDUS MAGNUS, ANGLO SAXONUM *Rex* ' *doctiffimus, ad exemplar* JUNIANUM *defcriptam edidit* WILLI- ' ELMUS ELSTOB, *A. M. et Coll. Univ. Socius. Oxoniæ, e Theatro* ' *Sheldoniano A. D.* MDCIC.'

Mr. Elftob was particularly ufeful to his fifter, in the great advances fhe made in literature, as likewife in her publications. This fhe teftifies, both in her preface to the edition of the Saxon Homily, and in the MS. Life of her brother. But concerning her, I muft now fubjoin fome few Memoirs, and the rather, be-caufe, as fhe was living when Mr. Ballard publifhed his *Memoirs of the learned Ladies of Great Britain,* anno 1752, there is no account of her in that work. Mr. Ballard otherwife was well acquainted with her, correfponded with her, and had the higheft efteem for her on account of her uncommon learning and ac-complifhments, and doubtlefs would have done all proper honour to her memory on that occafion.

She was born in the parifh of St. Nicholas, in Newcaftle upon Tyne, September 29, 1683, fo that fhe was ten years younger than her brother. Her mother, who was a great admirer of learning, efpecially in her own fex, obferved the particular fond-

---

[1] See Mr. Ballard's Pref. p. 47.
[2] With which the learned world were favoured in 1773, by the Hon. Daines Bar-rington. See Ballard's Preface, and alfo Wanley's Catalogue of Saxon MSS. p. 85. and Mrs. Elftob's Preface to Homily on St. Gregory's Day, p. 6.

nefs which her daughter had for books, and omitted nothing that might tend to her improvement fo long as she lived; but alas! she was fo unfortunate as to lofe her mother when she was about eight years of age, and had but juft gone through her Accidence and Grammar. A ftop was now put to her progrefs for a time, through a vulgar miftaken notion of her guardian, *that one Tongue was enough for a woman.* However, the force of natural inclination ftill carried her to improve her mind in the beft manner she could, and as her propenfity was ftrong towards languages, she with much difficulty obtained leave to learn the French tongue. But her fituation in this refpect was happily much altered when she went to live with her brother, who, being impreffed with more liberal fentiments concerning the education of women, very joyfully affifted and encouraged her in her ftudies for the whole time he lived. Under his eye, she tranflated and publifhed an *Effay on Glory*, written in French by the celebrated Mademoifelle de Scudery. But what characterizes Mrs. Elftob moft, she, as she intimates in her Dedication to the Saxon Homily, was the firft English woman that had ever attempted that ancient and obfolete language, and I fuppofe is alfo the laft. But she was an excellent linguift in other refpects, being not only miftrefs of her own and the Latin tongue [1], but alfo of feven other languages. And she owed all her fkill in the learned tongues, except what may be afcribed to her own diligence and application, to her brother. She was withal a good antiquary and divine, as appears evidently from her works, which I muft now recite.

She publifhed an English-Saxon Homily on the Birth-day, that is, the Death-day, of St. Gregory, anciently ufed in the English-Saxon church, giving an account of the converfion of the English

[1] Epift. Fratris ad eam citat. fuprà.

from

from Paganifm to Chriftianity, tranflated into modern Englifh, with notes, &c. London, 1709. It is a pompous book, in large octavo, with a fine frontifpiece, headpieces, tailpieces, and blooming letters. She dedicates her work, which was printed by fubfcription, to queen Anne. Mr. Thorefby, in the Ducatus Leod. p. 129, gives notice of this intended publication [1], and there ftyles her the *juftly celebrated Saxon Nymph.* Her preface, which is indeed an excellent and learned performance, was particularly ferviceable to Mr. Ballard, who has made good ufe of it, in evincing the advantages of the Anglo-Saxon literature, and ingenuoufly acknowledges it [2].

A. D. 1715, fhe printed ' The Rudiments of Grammar for ' the Englifh Saxon tongue, firft given in Englifh [3]; with an ' Apology for the Study of Northern Antiquities,' 4to. It was intended to be prefented to the princefs Sophia; but as fhe died before it made its appearance, it is dedicated to the late queen Caroline, then princefs of Wales. The Apology is addreffed to the moft learned Dr. Hickes.

The Life of her brother and of herfelf, written at the requeft of Mr. Ballard, have been noticed above; wherefore I omit them here, only remarking, that it appears from a note of Mr. Ballard's, on the former piece, that fhe had drawn up the pedigree of her family, very curioufly, upon vellum; fhewing, that, by the maternal fide, the *Elftobs* were defcended from the old kings or princes of Wales; in the middle there was a column, on the top of which ftood king Brockmail, on one fide the paternal, and on the other maternal defcents. It was in the earl of Oxford's

---

[1] Her work was publifhed before Mr. Thorefby's, his Dedication bearing date 1714; but, I prefume, he had written this paffage, before her book, to which he was a fubfcriber, was publifhed.

[2] See his MS. Preface to Orofius.

[3] Dr. Hickes's labours on the fubject being in Latin.

library.

library. Moreover, she tells us in her own life, that she had taken an exact copy of the *Textus Roffensis* upon vellum, ' now ' in the library of that great and generous encourager of learn- ' ing, the late right honourable the earl of Oxford.' My friend Mr. Astle has now a MS. volume in his collection, chiefly in her hand-writing, but partly in that of her brother, intituled, *Col- lectanea quædam Anglo-Saxonica, e Codd. MSS. hinc inde congesta.* And in this original *Textus Roffensis* there is the Saxon alphabet on the reverse of the second folio signed *E. E.* which I presume must be her name.

It appears also from a word of her brother's, that she had joined with him in preparing and adorning an edition of Gregory's Pastoral '; a work which, I imagine, was intended to include both the original, and the Saxon version of it.   And she in- forms us herself, in her Life, that ' she had transcribed all the ' Hymns from an ancient MS. belonging to the church of ' Sarum.'

In the Preface to the Anglo-Saxon Grammar, p. 11. she speaks of a work of a larger extent, in which she was engaged, and which had *amply experienced Dr.* HICKES's *encouragement.*   This was a Saxon Homilarium, or a collection of the English Saxon Homilies of Ælfric, archbishop of Canterbury.   It was a noble though unsuccesful enterprize, and indeed her most capital un- dertaking.   Mr. Ballard gives the following account of it.   ' Dr. ' Hickes, well knowing the great use which those Homilies had ' been of, and still might be, to the church of England, designed ' to publish, among other Saxon tracts, a volume of Saxon ' Homilies.   But then he tells us ², that though for want of ' further encouragement he could not carry on any one of those

---

' Epist. Fratris ad eam supra laudata.
² Hickes's Dedication to the first volume of his Sermons.

' designs,

' defigns, yet it was no fmall pleafure to him, to fee one of the
' moft confiderable of them attempted, with fo much fuccefs,
' by Mrs. Elizabeth Elftob, " who," adds he, " with incredible
" induftry hath furnifhed a Saxon HOMILARIUM, or a Collection
" of the Englifh-Saxon Homilies of Alfric, archbifhop of Can-
" terbury, which fhe hath tranflated, and adorned with learned
" and ufeful notes ', and for the printing of which fhe hath
" publifhed propofals; and I cannot but wifh that for her own
" fake, as well as for the advancement of the Septentrional learn-
" ing, and for the honour of our Englifh-Saxon anceftors, the
" fervice of the Church of England, the credit of our country,
" and the honour of her fex, that learned and moft ftudious
" gentlewoman may find fuch encouragement as fhe and her
" great undertaking deferve." This work was begun printing
' in a very pompous folio at the theatre in Oxon (and five or
' more of the Homilies were wrought off in a very beautiful
' manner), and was to have born the following title. *The Englifh*
' *Saxon Homilies of* ÆLFRIC, *archbifhop of* CANTERBURY, *who*
' *flourifhed in the latter end of the tenth century, and the beginning*
' *of the eleventh. Being a Courfe of Sermons collected out of the*
' *Writings of the ancient* LATIN *Fathers, containing the Doctrines,*
' *&c. of the Church of* ENGLAND *before the* NORMAN *Conqueft,*
' *and fhewing its purity from many of thofe Popifh innovations and*
' *corruptions which were afterwards introduced into the Church.*
' *Now firft printed and tranflated into the language of the prefent*
' *times, by* ELIRABETH ELSTOB [2].'

This elogium of Mrs. Elftob, and her undertaking, by fo great
a man, and a perfon fo well verfed in the fubject as Dr. Hickes,
redounds infinitely to the lady's honour; the defign, however,
though fo profperoufly begun, and even fo far advanced, proved

---

[1] And, as fhe mentions in her own Life, had added the various readings.
[2] Ballard's MS. Preface to Orofius, penes Epifc. Cirkol.

abortive,

abortive, for the work was never publifhed, for want, I imagine of encouragement; what is become of the MS. I have not at prefent learned.

But this excellent woman, her profound learning, and maf-culine abilities notwithftanding, was very unfortunate in life. After the death of her brother, and the ill fuccefs of her ftudies, fhe was obliged to depend upon her friends for fubfiftence, but did not meet with that generofity fhe might reafonably expect; bifhop Smalridge being the only perfon from whom fhe received any relief. After being fupported by his friendly hand for a while, fhe at laft could not bear the thoughts of continuing a burthen to one who was not very opulent himfelf; and being fhocked with the cold refpect of fome, and the haughty fcorn of others, fhe determined to retire to a place unknown, and to try to get her bread by teaching children to read and work, and fhe fettled for that purpofe at Evefham in Worcefterfhire.

At Evefham fhe led at firft but an uncomfortable and penurious life; but growing acquainted afterwards with the gentry of the town, her affairs mended, but ftill fhe fcarce had time to eat, much lefs for ftudy [1]. She became known after this to Mr. Ballard [2], whom I have fo often mentioned; and about the year

1733,

[1] Her own account of her fituation at Evefham goes thus: ' I had feveral other ' defigns, but was unhappily hindered by a neceffity of getting my bread, which, ' with much difficulty, labour, and ill health, I have endeavoured to do for many ' years, with very indifferent fuccefs. If it had not been that Almighty God was ' gracioufly pleafed to raife me up lately fome gracious and good friends, I could ' not have fubfifted; to whom I always was, and will, by the grace of God, be ' moft grateful.' MS. Life.

[2] Ballard's Memoirs, p. 249. This Mr. Ballard was a moft extraordinary perfon: he was bred in low life, a woman's taylor, at Campden, in Gloucefterfhire, but having a turn for letters, and in particular towards the Saxon learning, he became acquainted, from a fimilarity of ftudy with Mrs. Elftob, after fhe was fettled at Evefham. By the affiftance of the Rev. Mr. Talbot, vicar of Keinton, in War-wickfhire, and a recommendation to the Prefident of Magdalen College, Oxon, he

removed

1733, one Mrs. Capon, the wife of a clergyman of French extraction, who kept a private boarding school at Stanton, in Gloucestershire, and was herself a person of literature, enquired of him after her, and being informed of the place of her abode, made her a visit. Mrs. Capon, not being in circumstances to assist her herself, wrote a circular letter to her friends, in order to promote a subscription in her behalf. This letter, which was extremely well written, describing her merit, her extensive learning, her printed works, her ease and affluence till her brother's death, her multiplied distresses afterwards, and the meekness and patience with which she bore them, had the desired effect, and an annuity of twenty guineas was raised for her. This enabled her to keep an assistant, by which means she could again taste of that food of the mind, from which she had been so long obliged to fast. A lady, soon after, shewed Mrs. Capon's letter to queen Caroline, who, recollecting her name [1], and delighted with the opportunity of taking such eminent merit into her protection, said, she would allow her twenty pounds *per annum*; but, adds she, as she is so proper to be mistress of a boarding school for young ladies of a higher rank, I will, instead of an annual allowance, send her one hundred pounds now, and repeat the same at the end of every five years. On the death of queen Caroline, anno 1737, a most unlucky event in appearance for poor Mrs. Elstob, she was seasonably recommended to the present dutchess dowager of Portland; and her grace, to whose father, the earl of Oxford, she had been well known, was pleased of her goodness to appoint her governess to her children; this was

---

removed to that University. The President appointed him one of the eight clerks of his college, which furnished him with chambers and commons; and thus being a *Gremial*, he was afterwards elected, by the procurement of the President, one of the Beadles of the University. See more of him in the Anecdotes of Bowyer, pp. 10. 500.

[1] On account of the Dedication beforementioned.

in

in the year 1739; and from this period, the letters fhe wrote to
Mr. Ballard, which are now in the Bodleian Library, are obferved to have a more fprightly turn, and fhe feems to have been
exceedingly happy in her fituation. To be fhort, fhe died in
an advanced age, in her Grace's fervice, May 30, 1756, and
was buried at St. Margaret's, Weftminfter. I am obliged to my
much efteemed friend, Mr. Thomas Seward, refidentiary of
Lichfield, for the above very particular account of the latter part
of Mrs. Elftob's life; and as this gentleman knew both her and
Mrs. Capon perfonally, and was one of the fubfcribers above-
mentioned, the narrative may be depended upon [1].

I proceed now to fpeak of the remaining publications of the
Textus Roffenfis :

Dr. Harris's Hiftory of Kent was publifhed, anno 1719, as
was mentioned. He has printed feveral extracts from the *Textus*,
as has been already noted, but always gives the Saxon in the
common type ; I think nothing appears here, but what had been
already publifhed, except that p. 32. he gives us the Arabick numeral characters from it, as they appear on the top of each leaf,
or each other page, which he fuppofes to be of the fame age
with the book itfelf, which might be finifhed, as he conjectures,
about anno 1120 [2]. This I think to be a point very doubtful,
fince the numerals that appear in the book, where they are often
applied, are always Roman, a ftrong prefumption, that thefe
characters on the top of the leaves have been added fince. However, the Doctor has added thefe numeral characters to Mrs.
Elftob's alphabet on the reverfe of the fecond folio in the original,
in his own hand-writing, with this note : *This fhews thefe Arabic
characters to have been ufed here about the year 1115, when Ernulfus was confecrated* [3].

[1] Some farther particulars both of Mrs. Elftob and her brother may be feen in
the Anecdotes of Bowyer, pp. 11. 48. 110. 216. 498. 502. 528.
[2] See what has been faid above on this fubject.
[3] See what has been faid upon this.

I have

I have heard that a bad accident happened to our MS. at this time, which endangered the entire lofs of it. Being carried by water from Rochefter to London, and back again, the book by fome means or other fell in its return into the water, but was happily recovered, and without much damage[1]; for when I faw it, about the year 1742, by the favour of the late archbifhop Herring, who was then bifhop of Bangor and dean of Rochefter, it was in a very good condition, being a fmall quarto on vellum, bound in red[2]. The book has been in perils both by land and water, and I prefume this laft efcape will prove a fufficient warning to the dean and chapter, not to fuffer it to go any more out of their cuftody.

Upon the return of the book to its abode at Rochefter, the learned Mr. John Johnfon[3], rector of Cranbrook, in Kent, had recourfe to it; thefe are his words: ' Since my tranflation of ' thofe Laws (of Wihfred king of Kent) was printed off, I was ' informed that this *Textus* was reftored to its place of refidence, ' and I had the favour of perufing it; but I found no variation ' of moment, but what Mr. Somner had taken notice of in his ' written notes; yet, by infpecting the original, I was able to ' diftinguifh between Mr. Somner's conjectural emendations, and ' thofe which he made from the text itfelf[4].' Mr. Johnfon's Collection of Laws, &c. came out, anno 1720, in 2 vols. 8vo.

A. D. 1720, Mr. Hearne, the famous Oxford Antiquary, publifhed Sir Edward Dering's tranfcript in 8vo. by fubfcription, at 5s. for the fmall, and 10s. for the large paper. The tranfcript had lain in the library at Surenden-Dering, from A. D. 1632,

---

[1] ' The MS. itfelf,' fays Mr. Johnfon, who faw it after this difafter, ' is in a very ' fair hand, and well preferved, fave where it is *tarnifhed by the falt-water* it took ' in its late travels.' Pref. to Collection of Laws, &c. p. iv.

[2] It has been new bound fince Dr. Harris ufed it, probably after its recovery from the deep.

[3] Of whom a particular account will be annexed to this Differtation.

[4] Johnfon's Preface to his Collection of Laws, &c. p. iii.

and

and from thence the late John Anftis, Efq. Garter King at Arms,
my very worthy friend, borrowed it for Mr. Hearne of the late
Sir Edward Dering, a gentleman for whom I fhall always profefs
the higheft efteem.   The MS. does not now appear in the library, having never been returned by thefe gentlemen; this,
however, is not a thing of much confequence; fince the firft
Baronet always intended his MS. for publication, and as it is
now printed, and we can perfectly rely upon this editor for the
accuracy of his performance[1].   Mr. Hearne had both Sir Edward Dering's leave for the publication, and that of the late
Bifhop Atterbury, which laft was procured for him by Mr. Anftis.
The editor has not printed the whole of Sir Edward Dering's
tranfcript, for he has omitted fome things, either already publifhed, or that might be publifhed by others, confining himfelf
chiefly to fuch matters as might relate *ad rem diplomaticam*[2].
Thus, for example, he has omitted the *Judicia Civitatis Lundoniæ*,
becaufe they are almoft all extant in Brompton, and were intended to be inferted by Dr. Wilkins in his edition of the *Legg.
Anglo-Saxon*.   It is a miftake, therefore, in Bifhop Tanner, to fay,
that the *whole Textus Roffenfis* was printed by Mr. Hearne[3].   There
were fome additions made by Sir Edward in the margin of his
tranfcript; concerning thefe, the editor tells us, left they fhould
be thought an objection to the authority of the copy, ‘ Exfcrip-
‘ torem fuiffe virum eruditiffimum, ipfique nulla privati emo-
‘ lumenti fpe fuiffe decretum annotationes paullo prolixiores ac
‘ uberiores in regiftrum hoc fcribere[4].’   But we do not find
that Sir Edward made any great advances in the defign of a com-
mentary; Mr. Hearne goes on, ‘ Adeo ut notulæ marginales

---

[1] The inftrument which the accurate Sir William Blackftone has given us, p. iv.
of his Introduction to his fuperb edition of Magna Charta, &c. is copied from
Hearne's edition.
[2] Hearne's Præf. p. vii.
[3] Tanner's Biblioth. p. 265.
[4] Hearne's Præf. p. xiii.

‘ (e quarum

' (e quarum fane numero funt clypei cum crucibus decuffatis),
' lineæque fub aliquibus vocibus in textu dudæ, funt exfcriptoris;
' quas omnes ideo adjungendas cenfuimus, ne eruditorum quif-
' quam fidem noftram fufpedam haberet, &c.' As to thefe
fhields *cum crucibus decuffatis*, they are the arms of Sir Edward
Dering, which Mr. Hearne feems not to be aware of; for the
coat of this family is O. a faltire S. and the fhields are always
put againft thofe places where mention is made of the name of
Dering, or of perfons that might probably belong to his family,
and in order to infinuate the fame: fee pp. 184, 185. 192. 200.
218. 235.

I would further note, that the tranfcript, procured by the
Elftobs, contains fomething more than this of Sir Edward. There
you have the genealogiés printed by Dr. Gale; the names of the
popes and emperors, the bifhops of Jerufalem, the bifhops of
Alexandria, the bifhops of Antioch, the archbifhops of Canterbury, the bifhops of Rochefter, printed by Mr. Wharton, and
the bifhops of the feveral fees in England. That chafm in
Hearne, p. 127, is fupplied, as likewife are all the other chafms;
a large Saxon inftrument beginning paða ꝼe biꝛcop ʒaðꝑine, &c.
occurs alfo in Elftob's tranfcript; and the catalogue of books,
which is fo fhort in Hearne, p. 234, extends here to many
pages.

My late good friend the very worthy and learned Dr. John
Denne, archdeacon of Rochefter, has been at the pains of collating his copy of Mr. Hearne's edition with the original MS.
throughout. He has noted where every leaf of the original
begins, the true readings of the MS. in feveral places, an omiffion
here and there, and has tranfcribed the marginal additions that
appear in the original by feveral later hands, as Mr. Lambard,
Sir Edward Dering, &c. The Doctor has moreover noted with
the utmoft care and diligence in what other MSS. the feveral
inftruments treafured up in this chartulary are alfo to be found,

as

as in the *Regiſtrum Temp. Roff.* and the Cotton Library, which makes his book of greatly more value than the naked edition of Mr. Hearne. The Doctor was afterwards pleaſed to give me leave to tranſcribe into my copy all the annotations here mentioned, together with the references as above, which I got done by a very careful hand, the Rev. Mr. Richard Huſband, minor canon of Rocheſter, my reſpectable friend.

A. D. 1721, Dr. Wilkins's edition of the *Anglo-Saxon* Laws came out in folio. He has compared the Laws of Ethelbert, Hlothere, and Eadric, with our MS. and ſupplied the defects and chaſms in De Laet's verſion; what other uſe ne has made of the original, may be ſeen in his Preface.

A. D. 1737. This gentleman publiſhed *Concilia Magnæ Britanniæ*, &c. in 4 volumes, folio; and in the firſt volume are many articles from Spelman's former edition, compared with the *Textus*, and chiefly, as I think, by Mr. Somner, as may be collected from the Doctor's Preface, p. iii. compared with Biſhop Kennet's Life of Somner, p. 89.

COROLLARY.

The *Textus Roffenſis* is doubtleſs in very ſafe and good hands; but if, by any accident, an unexpected misfortune ſhould now happen to it, ſufficient care has been taken to perpetuate it, by the ſeveral publications above-mentioned; the tranſcripts [1] made by the Elſtobs, and the collation made by Dr. Denne, of which laſt there are at preſent two copies. However, whereas Dr. Wilkins ſays, ' Maxime venerandum hoc monumentum antiquitatis ' in ſummum reipublicæ literariæ commodum typis expreſſum ' extat [2];' this is not ſtrictly true, ſome parts of the MS. having not been yet *printed*; but they are nevertheleſs ſecured by the tranſcripts.   SAMUEL PEGGE.

---

[1] I expreſs it plurally, on account of Mrs. Elſtob's own tranſcript on vellum, mentioned above.

[2] Dr. Wilkins, Præf. ad Tanner's Biblioth p. xliv.

Biographical Anecdotes of Mr. JOHNSON.

JOHN JOHNSON, the celebrated author of a fingular doctrine concerning the Euchariſt, was the ſon of Mr. Thomas Johnſon, vicar of Frindſbury, in Kent, by Mary his wife, daughter of the rev. Mr. Francis Drayton, rector of Little Chart, in the ſame county. He was born December 30, 1662; and his father dying when he was ſcarcely four years old, and his mother retiring to the country, he was put to the king's ſchool there, under Mr. Lovejoy, and at little more than 15 years old admitted of Magdalen College, Cambridge, $167\frac{7}{8}$. He proceeded B. A. $168\frac{1}{2}$; and was ſoon after nominated, by the dean and chapter of Canterbury, to one of archbiſhop Parker's ſcholarſhips in Corpus Chriſti or Bene't College in the ſame univerſity, where he took the degree of M. A. 1685. Soon after, he entered into deacon's orders, and became curate to Mr. Thomas Hondras, at Hardres near Canterbury, and was ordained prieſt by biſhop Sprat, in Henry VII's chapel, 1686. Archbiſhop Sancroft collated him to the vicarage of Boughton under Blean, and allowed him to hold by ſequeſtration the adjoining vicarage or Hernhill, both which churches he ſupplied himſelf every Sunday. In 1689 he married Margaret daughter of Thomas Jenkin, gent. of the Iſle of Thanet, and ſiſter to the rev. Dr. Robert Jenkin, Maſter of St. John's College, Cambridge, and to the rev. Mr. Henry Jenkin, rector of Tilney in Norfolk. About this time, one Sale, who had forged letters of orders, and taking advan-

F   tage

tage of the interval between the fufpenfion of archbifhop Sancroft, and confecration of archbifhop Tillotfon, to find out the
livings held by fequeftration only, had got the broad feal for
one for himfelf and another for his father; Mr. Jenkin took
inftitution to Hernhill, and the archbifhop, being then only fuf-
pended *ab officio* and not *a beneficio*, prefented him to it, to
which he was inftituted, 1689, by Dr. Oxenden, vicar-general
to the archbifhop, but then to the dean and chapter of Canterbury, guardians of the fpiritualities during the fufpenfions; but
as the living had been held by fequeftration fo long as to be lapfed
to the crown, he found it neceffary to take out the broad feal,
1690.   In 1697 archbifhop Tenifon prefented him to the vicarage of St. John's Margate, and of Appledore, on the edge of
Romney Marfh, but he chofe to hold the firft by fequeftration
only.   Here, for the benefit of educating his two fons, he took
in two or three boarders, the fons of particular friends; but,
finding he could not attend his little fchool and his great curacy,
and his ftudies, in a manner fatisfactory to himfelf, he refigned
Margate, and fettled at Appledore, 1703.   When his eldeft fon
went before the age of 15 to the Univerfity, 1705, he difmiffed
his boarders, fending his other fon to fchool to qualify him for
bufinefs. But the marfhy air brought on a fevere illnefs on
himfelf and family.   He obtained the vicarage of Cranbrook
of the archbifhop, 1707, and there he continued to his death,
keeping a curate both there and at Appledore. In the years 1710
and 1713, he was chofen proctor in convocation for the diocefe
of Canterbury, which introduced him to the acquaintance of the
moft eminent clergy of the province.   A little before he left
Appledore, he printed feveral Tracts, to which he declined put-
ting his name till they came to a fecond edition.   The firft was
a Paraphrafe, with notes, on the Pfalms, according to the tranflation in the Common Prayer Book, intituled, " Holy David and

                                                                " his

" his old English Tranflation cleared, 1706;" he next printed " The
" Clergyman's Vade Mecum, 1708," which went through a 5th
edition, 1727; the fecond part, 1709, had a third edition. In 1710
he wrote and publifhed " Propitiatory Oblations in the holy Eu-
" charift truly ftated and defended from fcripture, and antiquity,
" and the common fervice of the Church of England." He was
quickly known to be the author of this book, which being attackt
by Dr. Wife of Canterbury, put the author quite out of favour
at Lambeth during the reft of archbifhop Tenifon's time. But this
ferved but to induce him to handle the argument more at large,
and prove the Eucharift to be a true and proper facrifice from
the authority of fcripture and the teftimony of the antient
fathers and liturgies of the firft, fourth, or fifth centuries after
Chrift. This he did in " The unbloody facrifice and altar un-
" veiled and fupported. In which the nature of the Eucharift
" is explained according to the fentiments of the Chriftian
" church in the four firft centuries, proving that the Eucharift
" is a proper material facrifice; that it is both euchariftic and
" propitiatory; that it is to be offered by proper officers; that the
" oblation is to be made on a proper altar; that it is to be con-
" fumed by manducation : to which is added, a proof that what
" our Saviour fpeaks concerning eating his flefh, and drinking
" his blood, in the fixth chapter of St. John's Gofpel, is prin-
" cipally meant of the Eucharift. With a prefatory epiftle to
" the Lord Bifhop of Norwich, animadverting on Dr. Wife's book,
" which he calls the Chriftian Eucharift ftated, and fome
" Reflections on a ftitched book, intituled, an Anfwer to the
" Exceptions made againft the Lord Bifhop of Oxford's Charge.
" Part I." To this he fet his name. The fecond part was publifhed 1717, with anfwers to a frefh reply of Dr. Wife;
another by Mr. Lewis, his fucceffor at Margate; and a third by
Mr. Pfatty, a Lutheran Divine, tutor to the prince of Wertemberg,

who

who took upon him to be moderator in this controverfy. His next publication was " A Collection of Ecclefiaftical Laws, Canons," &c. in two volumes, 8vo. In 1724, the firft volume of his " Unbloody Sacrifice" was re-printed, with a Reply to Dr. Rymer's " General Reprefentation of Revealed Religion, 1723," and " The Doctrine of the Euchariſt ſtated, 1720;" as alfo to the 12th of Dr. Clarke's XVII Sermons. His " Primitive Communicant," " Explanation of Daniel's LXX Weeks, a Seimon at Canterbury " fchool-feaſt, with a Preface, ſhewing, that no letters were " before Mofes," were publiſhed after his deceaſe, with his Life, by his friend Mr. Thomas Brett, 1748, as were alfo ſome other poſthumous pieces.

Mr. Johnfon had two fons and three daughters. His eldeſt daughter died in her infancy : his youngeſt fon foon after he had bound him apprentice to Mr. Knaplock, his bookfeller ; and a few years after, his youngeſt daughter died in the prime of life. His eldeſt fon was fellow of St. John's College, Cambridge, where he took the degree of Batchelor of Divinity, and was prefented by the Univerfity to the living of Standiſh, in the county of Lancafter, worth 500l. *per annum*; but before he had enjoyed it one whole year, he had the misfortune to break his leg, which threw him into a fever, of which he died in a few days, about Chriſtmas, 1723. Mr. Johnfon could not overcome this fevere ſtroke, though he intermitted not his ſtudies, nor the duties of his office : yet from this time his ſtrength vifibly decayed, and he was afflicted with a ſhoitnefs of breath, which increafed on him till he died, about two years after his fon, Dec. 15, 1725, having juſt reached the 63d year of his age. He was buried in the church-yard of Cranbrook, cloſe to the veſtry-wall. Over his grave is erected a handſome altar monument of grey marble, with this infcription: *John Johnfon, Vicar*; but on the other

fide

ſide of the wall within the veſtry is the following inſcription on a mural monument of white marble.

Extra hunc parietem
ſub tumulo lapideo requieſcit
JOANNES JOHNSON, A. M.
per annos octodecim hujus eccleſiæ paſtor,
morum caſtitate, ingenii acumine,
interioribus & reconditis literis ornatiſſimus,
filius reverendi Thomæ Johnſon
de Frindſbury in diocæſi Roffenſ. vicariæ,
et Mariæ filiæ reverendi Franciſci Drayton
Chart Parvæ hujus diocæſeos rectoris.
Uxorem habuit Margaretam,
filiam Thomæ Jenkin,
in inſula de Thanet generoſi,
de qua quinque ſuſcepit liberos,
quorum quatuor ſuperſtitit,
viz. Margaretæ incunabulis mortuæ,
Thomæ Londini ſepulto,
Alteri Margaretæ ſiniſtra patris dormienti
Joanni S. T. B. de Standiſh
in comitatu Lancaſtrienſi rectori,
Paternæ virtutis, ingenii & eruditionis
exemplari,
cujus poſt mortem cum fere per biennium
ægre ſuſpiria duxiſſet
animam ſpei beatæ immortalitatis plenam
Deo reſtituit 15° die Decembris,
A. D. 1725, ætatis 63.
Eccleſiæ Anglicanæ pugil, ſchiſmatis debellator
Occidit — ſi plura quæris ſcripta mortui verſato.
Pientiſſima filia Maria Johnſon poſuit.

The following is the character drawn of him by his friend and biographer Dr. Brett.

" As no prieſt was more careful and diligent to inſtruct thoſe committed to his care in the knowledge of their duty by his ſermons, ſo was he no leſs careful to inſtruct them by his

example

example in a regular Chriftian life. None was better beloved by his parifhioners, and all who had the happinefs of his acquaintance; and when we confider his learning, and his critical fkill in the languages proper, not to fay neceffary, for a divine, his great and extenfive knowledge of the canons and conftitutions of the Chriftian Church, and the cuftoms and difcipline in the feveral ages, from the firft planting of the gofpel downward to our own times, and his capacity to teach them, and alfo his exemplary life and converfation, we may as juftly fay of him what was faid of the learned Mr. Bingham, in Mift's Journal, January 4, 172¾. *Qui patriarchatum in ecclefia meruit parochus obiit.* His converfation was eafy and chearful, and very improving. If any one departed out of his company without learning fomething from him, it was his own fault. He was very diligent in the performing of all parochial duties: he read prayers every morning in his parifh church; when he was at home, he preached twice every Sunday; frequently inftructed children in the Catechifm; adminiftered the Holy Euchariſt every month; was diligent in vifiting the fick, or any other that needed his ghoftly advice or prayers; and, in a word, ufed that faithful diligence which he promifed when he was admitted into the order of priefthood. He was a dutiful fon, a loving hufband, a tender and careful father, an obliging kind friend, and confcientioufly careful to difcharge his duty in every relation."

The following anecdote the late Mr. Jones of Welwyn had from fome of his parifhioners; which is confirmed by the large baptiftery ftill fubfifting in Cranbrook church. " Mr. Johnfon, when he came to refide at Cranbrook, finding that many of the inhabitants were Anabaptifts, or rather *Baptifts*, as they affected to ftyle themfelves; ufed many arguments to perfuade them to con-

3   " form

form to the church. They made a great objection to the practice of *sprinkling* in baptism; and said, that the church in a manner excluded them from her communion in refusing to baptize by immersion. Mr. Johnson readily allowed the propriety of that practice, according to the original institution; and, to remove this difficulty, caused a large baptistery to be erected in the church. Upon this, most of the Anabaptists in his parish were *dipped,* &c. and were received into the church, to which they owned they had no farther objection. And Mr. Johnson, on his part, assured them he had no objection to the practice of *dipping*; and from that time they lived in perfect harmony together. R. W."

He was sensible that the Church of England allowed Immersion, at the same time that it allowed also Aspersion; and he well knew that he was at liberty to admit adult persons into the fellowship of this church by the ceremony of dipping, &c.

The women had a grave matron (called a Deaconess), to attend their baptism. And all was conducted with great decency.

They had asked him where they should find room? He readily answered, There is a large chancel at liberty.

Those that came over to the established communion, upon his shewing them this civility and condescension, assembled by his direction in the chancel to attend divine service; for several of them were unsupplied with seats in the body of the church.

This anecdote entirely removes the uncharitable supposition of Mr. Johnson's Biographer Dr. Brett, who, after saying that he was much loved and highly esteemed by all his parishioners at Cranbrook who were friends to the Church of England as by law established, adds, " But as there were many dissenters of all ' denominations in that place, and some who, though they fre- " quented the church, yet seemed to like Dissenters better than

" Church-

"Churchmen, I cannot fay how they loved or efteemed him.
"However, his life and converfation was fuch that even they
"could find nothing in him to difpleafe them, except his known
"affection to the Church of England. Some of thefe favourers
"of the Diffenters endeavoured to make him uneafy, and to fpirit
"up a party in the church againft him; but failed in their de-
"figns: his friends were too many for them."

The fucceffor in that vicarage was not of fo obliging a temper
as Mr. Johnfon; and the Baptiftery is fuffered to run to ruin, or
is confiderably impaired.

A N E C D O T E S *inferted in the Regifter of* CRANBROOK, *by the Reverend* JOHN JOHNSON, *Vicar.*

"MEMORANDUM.

HIS grace William archbifhop of Canterbury did, at the requeft of John Johnfon, Vicar of Cranbrook, adminifter confirmation at this place to above thirteen hundred perfons, of which one third at leaft were of this parifh, on Sunday, June 24th, being St. John Baptift's Feaft, anno Domini 1716. There had been no confirmation here in 28 years before, that is, fince the fatal year 1688, when the moft reverend archbifhop Sancroft, of pious memory, being difcharged from his cuftody in the Tower, upon a trial in the King's Bench, fent bifhop Levinz (of Man Inf.) to perform the office of Confirmation throughout the diocefe, as he did bifhop Lloyd, of Norwich, fome years before. The fame archbifhop, of his own free motion, again adminiftered confirmation here on Sunday, June 21, 1724, to about thirteen hundred perfons, as his chaplain who attended him in the office told me; yet one of his grace's liverymen, who faid he numbered them, affirmed to me, that they were but twelve hundred."

G

Some

Some account of the Vicars of Cranbrook:

1503.   The firſt vicar of whom I can get any information, was Richard Wilſon; I have nothing of him but his name, and that from ſome pannels of glaſs in the vicarage-houſe in yellow paint, bearing date 1503.

1534.   Sir Hugh ap Rice returned a certificate into the Exchequer, giving an account of the value of this vicarage; upon which certificate this vicarage was taxed according to the rate at which it now ſtands in the king's books.

The copy of the certificate here follows:

" Cranbrook, the certificate of Sir Hugh ap Rice, vicar, theſe.

Firſt, a houſe with III roods of meadow, XIIIs. IIIId.

Item, III manſions worth yearly XIIIs. IIIId.

Item, one other manſion worth yearly xxd.

Item, Privy tithes, certain mills, with other caſual profits, worth yearly xIxl.

Item, IIII offering days VIIl. VIs.

Item, other caſual profits LIIIs. IIIId.

Sum', xxxl. VIIs. IIIId. whereof to be deducted for the pariſh prieſt x l.

Item, for the proxies to the archdeacon, VIIs.

Item, in quyt rents paid yearly xIIIId.

Sum deducted xl VIIIs. (4d. ſhould have been added) and ſo remained de claro xIxl. xIxs. VId."

This was drawn, A. D. 1534, and ſo it ſtandeth to this day.

This I took from a tranſcript of Mr. John Eaſon's, who is an officer of the firſt fruits and tenths.

1556. The pariſh is charged with a debt of 3l. due to Mr. Dr. Hues for books. I ſuppoſe this doctor being vicar, had procured a new ſet of books for the Popiſh ſervice. That this debt was ever paid does not appear.

1558. Richard Fletcher was made vicar here, the first Proteſtant predeceſſor that I meet with. He continued vicar 27 years, and lies buried on the north ſide of the church towards the upper end. He let a leaſe of the tenements belonging to this vicarage for 99 years to come, viz. from 1562 to 1661, and had it confirmed by the archbiſhop, and the dean and chapter of Canterbury. During all this time the vicar received but 13s. 4d. per annum for them. His ſon Richard was dean of Peterburgh, when the Queen of Scots was executed at Fotheringay Caſtle, and ſo diſplayed his loyalty on that occaſion, that he ſoon became biſhop of Briſtol; but not till his father was firſt dead, viz. 1589; therefore the monument in our chancel ſays not true, when it tells us, the father ſaw this ſon biſhop of Briſtol. He was afterterwards advanced to the ſee of Worceſter, and from thence to London. There he fell under the queen's diſpleaſure, and was ſuſpended; that he was reſtored before his death is not certain. Both he and his brother Gibs, the famous embaſſador to the Czar of Muſcovy, made Cranbrook vicarage their nurſery. Here their wives lay in, as appears by the regiſter. And even after the father's death, ſome of his ſon Gibs's children are buried here. Venner, the famous Puritan, preached here, whether as curate, or (as I rather ſuppoſe) lecturer, I know not. This was during the decline of Father Fletcher's life, and the diſgrace of archbiſhop Grindal. One would wonder, that Richard, afterwaids biſhop, did not uſe his intereſt with his father (if he brought him hither) or with the Vicar-general, to remove a man of ſuch ſorry notions and fantaſtic principles. Mr. Fletcher died 1585.

1585, Robert Roads, formerly preſident of St. John's College, Cambridge (where he was written) and continued here till 1589. His wife and he were buried in the ſame year.

1589,

1589, William Eddy fucceeded, and continued here in low circumftances till he died, 1616. I find no memorial of him, but that he was paid by the church-wardens for tranfcribing the regifter fairly from 1558 into the large old parchment book; and that he had the clerk's wages given him for calling the Pfalm, &c. Mr. Fletcher and he continued Vicars 58 years; and I am perfuaded, that, by thefe two long incumbances, the modus for Vicar's tithe was eftablifhed.

1616, Robert Abbot fucceeded. What relation he bore to the archbifhop of that name, I find not. But he was a man of eminent zeal and piety; and few, I am perfuaded, out-did him in learning and all commendable qualities. He defended the Church againft the Brownifts. I do not know that any could do it better. I have read his book, and cannot but wonder to find fuch a man here at that time of day. His Sermons, dedicated to the four principal families of the parifh; viz. Roberts, Baker's, Henly's, and Courthop's, fhew clearly, that he was a much greater man in polemical than in pulpit divinity. His " Young Man's Warning-piece" hath been more read than either of the other. It was publifhed 1635. The reafon of it was, one Rogers, a practifing Apothecary, who, from a very pious youth, became a very de-bauched man, and could not be prevailed upon to receive the facrament at Eafter, though he was to be excommunicated for that omiffion; and died foon after in great horrours and terrours. Abbot weathered out here in the worft of times till 1648 '. Then he was by the Rump Committee for Sequeftrations fent to another benefice, which he had long enjoyed together with this. At Smarden there was an Abbot; but, on comparing circumftances, and confidering Smarden books and ours, I remember fome years fince, I concluded that he of Smarden could not be the fame with this of Cranbrook.

' 1642-3, Walker's Sufferings of the Clergy, 183.

1648. John Williamfon, a ftrict Prefbyterian, was intruded here. The parifhioners engaged to make the vicarage 100l. *per annum* to him. To this end the churchwardens gathered the tithes and offerings, and the parifhioners made up the deficiencies; but this could not laft long.

1652. William Goodrick fucceeded him. He made himfelf remarkable by walking in the Market-place with his tithing-book in his hand, and his inkhorn hanging on his buttons, every Saturday, and dunning his parifhioners as he met them.

1662. John Cowper came in upon the Bartholomew Act, and fo difmiffed Goodrick, who yet for fome time kept a conventicle here. Cowper was a man of great wit and fine parts, but no œconomift: he left 4 or 5 children to fo many families in this country of the beft quality; who all accepted their feveral legacies.

1668. Mr. Charles Buck fucceeded; a gentleman of good fortune, and who lived here with great hofpitality; and was remarkable for his long fermons, till about 1694 it was thought neceffary that he fhould retire to London, for the cure of his head. From this time forward, Mr. Crowther the fchool-mafter ferved this cure till Mr. Buck died; viz. February 1706; though Mr. Buck returned to the vicarage two or three years before his death."

Mr. Johnfon has noticed he could never find out what relation his predeceffor Robert Abbot bore to the archbifhop of that name. His grace had an elder brother John, who was bifhop of Salifbury: is it likely that Robert was his fon [1]? Cranbrooke was a vicarage of fmall value to be fo long held by an archbifhop's nephew; it is plain, however, that he alfo long

[1] Not from Wood, who only fays that he left one fon or more. Ath. Ox. I. 431. The writer of his life in the Biographia Britannica follows Wood.

enjoyed

enjoyed another benefice with this living. It is mentioned in the Biographical Dictionary that bishop Abbot of Salisbury, who died the latter end of the year 1617, left one son and one daughter; and that he offended the archbishop by a second marriage. Robert was in 1648 removed from Cranbrooke by the committee for sequestrations; the reason assigned for it was, that he had taken another living, which by his own confession was inconsistent. So says Walker [1], adding, the reader will enquire further whether that be true or not. Having been, as Wood says, a frequent writer, we shall subjoin his account of him.

" Robert Abbot was of Cambridge, incorporated of Oxford, July 14, 1607. He was afterwards vicar of Cranbrooke, in Kent, a sider with the Presbyterians in the rebellion which began in 1642, was minister of Southwicke in Hampshire, and at length of St. Austin's church in Watling-street near St. Paul's cathedral in London, where, after he had been tumbled and tossed to and fro, he enjoyed himself quietly for some years in his old age. He hath written and published several things, among which are,

1. Four Sermons, &c. London, 1639, 8vo. dedicated to Walter Curle, bishop of Winchester, to whom he had been servant, and who then exhibited to his two sons, one at Oxford, and the other at Cambridge.

2. Tryal of the Church Forsakers, &c. on Heb. x. 23. London, 1639.

3. Milk for Babes, or a Mother's Catechism for her Children. London, 1646.

4. Three Sermons, printed in the former book.

5. A Christian Family builded by God, or Directions for Governors of Families. London, 1635, at which time the author was two years above the great climacterical year.

' Sufferings of the Clergy, p. 183.

Other

Other things he hath also publifhed (among which is, " Be Thankful, London, and her Sifters," a Sermon on Pfalm XXXI. 21. London, 1626), which for brevity fake I now omit '."

It appears from Le Neve's Fafti that a John Abbot was collated in 1712 to the 6th prebendal ftall in Canterbury cathedral, and that he was buried Sept. 1, 1615.

Strype, in his Life of Archbifhop Cranmer, p. 441. has obferved, that Cranbrooke was one of the large towns in the diocefe of Canterbury in which that prelate had noticed a learned man ought to be placed with a fufficient ftipend. At p. 274 of Strype's Life of Archbifhop Parker is a table of the rate of arms propofed to be found by the clergy of the diocefe of Canterbury; and in this table Cranbrooke is one of the places mentioned.

' Athen. Oxon. I. 431. Fafti I. 177.

END OF NUMBER XXV.

CPSIA information can be obtained at www.ICGtesting.com
Printed in the USA
LVOW07s1722220315

431568LV00021B/696/P

9 781170 244678